NATIONAL GEOGRAPHIC

Ladders

Catch the Light

BRIGHT LIGHTS HAVE A DARK SIDE

by Jennifer Boudart

A view of the United States at night reveals a dot-to-dot pattern of lights from coast to coast. The pattern of lights may seem beautiful, even comforting. But a growing number of scientists don't agree. Yet artificial light is immensely valuable to the human race.

Thomas Edison introduced the first practical light bulb in the late 1800s. This changed the way we spent our time. Life became safer after dark, and people did more after dark, too. Today an electric grid can light a room or an entire city.

Is too much night light a bad thing? People who study artificial light say light pollution may be hurting the environment and human health.

Studies show that light pollution is changing the rhythm of life on Earth. Pollution happens when a harmful substance enters the environment. Pollution can poison the air, land, and water. It can also harm plant and animal life.

In many places, light pollution and its effects are lighting up the night sky. Light pollution's effects take the form of sky glow, light trespass, and **glare.**

This satellite image of the United States shows how much light shines at night.

In the U. S., street lighting is less than 1% of electricity use. Yet there are plenty of street and alley lights in all cities.

70,000	Ann Arbor, MI
118,000	Philadelphia, PA
250,000	Chicago, IL
300,000	New York, NY

TOO MUCH LIGHT

People seem to want to light up the night. Often lights stay on all night long. Many lights are poorly designed for their purpose. They send too much light where it is *not* needed and not enough where it *is* needed.

Light shining up from the ground creates sky glow. It makes the night sky look bright when it should be dark. Sunlight, moonlight, and starlight bouncing off Earth are natural sources of sky glow. But most sky glow is caused by outdoor electric light, such as streetlights, lights shining through windows, and lights over public spaces.

All this electric light creates a glowing dome over cities and towns. The glow over big cities may be seen for hundreds of miles! Thus making stars and planets harder to see at night. Today people in cities usually can't see stars or other features of the night sky.

Light trespass is another form of light pollution. Trespass is also known as spill light. It happens when ground-level light shines into places where it isn't wanted. For example, lights are often kept on at night outside homes and in shopping centers for safety. This light shines into nearby houses and may bother the people who live there.

Glare is unshielded light shining straight out from its source, which can be dangerous. Glare can make it difficult to see in the dark. A flash of bright light can fill a person's entire field of view. The person will then have a hard time seeing obstacles while the eyes adjust. Groups of bright lights also make it hard to see obstacles, which can cause accidents.

Glare is especially dangerous for older people who are walking or driving at night. Glare is like other forms of light pollution. It can result from streetlights, parking lot lights, and moving vehicle lights.

The same lights that cause sky glow also cause light trespass. Trespass light can shine into the windows of nearby homes. People may not realize the effect this has on their neighbors.

Most billboards have lights at the bottom, so the light shines up. Most of that light escapes into the night sky. Placing lights on top of the billboard would reduce light pollution.

SOME LAWS TARGET LIGHT POLLUTION BY

- setting light curfews
- limiting light bulb brightness
- banning lights of a certain color

INDIVIDUALS CAN ALSO HELP BY

- using motion sensor lights
- buying light fixtures with shields to better direct light
- installing timer controls and dimmers

Light emits both day and night from buildings in large cities like Chicago, Illinois. The light of the night sky is barely visible until one travels many miles outside of the city.

HEALTH AND WELL-BEING

Is light pollution the price we need to pay in order to see well at night? Some people may think that only astronomers and stargazers worry about light pollution. Light pollution does impact observatories. Even a 10 percent increase in sky glow above natural levels affects telescope use. Telescopes do not work as well with sky glow. But that is only one problem. In our modern world, light pollution affects everyone. It impacts our health and well-being.

Long ago, ancient people looked to the stars to guide their travels. Since the invention of electric light, humans have turned away from the stars. And for many, the night sky has become unfamiliar.

In 1994, an earthquake knocked out power in Los Angeles. As the city grew dark, many people called 911 centers. They reported seeing a strange silvery cloud in the sky. They worried what they saw was related to the earthquake. But it was the Milky Way! These people had either never seen it or couldn't identify it.

The human body is programmed to respond to natural patterns of daylight and darkness. We are adapted to be **diurnal** creatures. We are mostly active during the day and at rest after dark. Many of our bodily functions, such as brain waves, follow a predictable pattern throughout the day and night. But the periods of day and night are changing.

Artificial light enables us to ignore our body rhythms. It also allows us to do activities later at night. Some animals are most active at night.

But humans are not **nocturnal.** The number of hours people can stay active is increasing because of artificial light. Previously, people were active only during hours of natural daylight. Depending on the season, there could be 10 to 14 hours of natural light. Now, 15.5 million people in the United States work night shifts and sleep during the day.

Americans are also finding it harder to fall asleep. Research shows that artificial light prevents the release of a hormone called *melatonin.* This hormone makes us feel sleepy and regulates our sleep/wake cycle.

Too much light at night can affect the natural rhythms and patterns of animal life.

Sea turtles have a hard time finding dark beaches needed for egg laying. When the eggs hatch, baby turtles look for light reflecting off the water. This helps them find the sea, but beachfront lights can confuse them.

Large metropolitan areas glow with lights at night. Medical research has started to show that being exposed to too much artificial light may be connected to sleep problems, obesity, and some forms of cancer.

The Milky Way as seen from
South Island, New Zealand.

26,000 LIGHT YEARS
distance from Earth to the center of the Milky Way

100 BILLION
stars in the Milky Way

13 BILLION YEARS
age of the oldest stars in the galaxy

OUR GALAXY

Earth and its solar system are part of the Milky Way Galaxy. From Earth, the center of the Milky Way is about 26,000 light years away. Interstellar dust (star dust) blocks clear telescope views of much of the Milky Way.

The Milky Way includes about 100 billion stars, maybe more. The oldest stars are in the middle of the galaxy. Such stars may be around 13 billion years old.

LIGHT POLLUTION SOLUTIONS

The International Dark-Sky Association (IDA) is working to reduce light pollution through "environmentally responsible outdoor lighting." IDA describes the night sky as "one half of the entire planet's natural environment" and says it should be considered a natural resource.

IDA has established the International Dark Sky Places program, which identifies International Dark Sky communities, parks, and reserves. These sites must be free of light pollution. Additionally landowners, cities, or towns must allow public access to these sites and run public education programs.

Many people cannot truly see the beauty of the night sky. Stars cannot shine through skyglow near a town or city. So turn off the lights and travel a little distance away. Head into the night. As many as 7,000 stars might be shining. And even the Milky Way is out there waiting for you!

Natural Bridges National Monument is in Utah. It is the world's first International Dark Sky Park.

Check In What is one way artificial light use affects people?

The Light Catchers

by Allan Woodrow
illustrated by Tuesday Mourning

The sky was as dark as night even though it was just past lunchtime. Why did they have to spend winter vacation with Grandpa Saul? Trevor would have liked to go some place warmer, brighter, and closer. Nine-year-old Trevor and his eleven-year-old sister, Alice, flew on a plane for 13 hours to get to Barrow, Alaska. Barrow is the northernmost city in the United States, and at this time of year, it is dark 24-hours a day.

Barrow, being so far north and so close to the North Pole, doesn't have regular days and nights. During the winter in Barrow, the sun sets in mid-November and doesn't rise again until the end of January. A visit to Barrow during this time was a **nocturnal** experience.

During the summer, it is the opposite. The sun does not set in Barrow for almost three months. Trevor would rather have daylight all day long than darkness all day long.

Now, snow fell outside, and it was icy cold. Winds blew so strong that Trevor expected them to lift the house and toss it away.

Making matters worse, Grandpa didn't like to keep many lights on; he said energy conservation was important. Trevor hated the dark because unfamiliar things lurked in the blackness.

Trevor was thinking those exact thoughts when the electricity went out and all the lights went with it, creating a total **blackout.**

Trevor's sense of hearing became sharper, and he heard footsteps creaking in the hall. He sensed something entering the room coming to get him, and he screamed.

"What's wrong?!" gasped Alice.

Trevor held on to something fleshy and bony. "I'm holding a monster!" he cried.

"You're holding my arm," said Alice, "Let go, you're hurting me!"
She turned on her flashlight and shone the beam of light at Trevor.

"Sorry," Trevor said, letting go of her arm.

"Grandpa told me to come get you," grumbled Alice, shaking her
arm. "Get a hold of yourself."

"You shouldn't sneak into my room like that," barked Trevor.

"I wasn't sneaking," said Alice. "Why haven't you unpacked?"

"I'll do it later," grumbled Trevor. "I feel like I should wear
everything I brought!"

Downstairs, Grandpa Saul waited on the floor
of the family room, but Trevor didn't see him
until Alice's flashlight found him. Alice and
Trevor sat on the floor next to him.

"Don't worry, these blackouts don't last
long," said Grandpa Saul.

"Blackouts are usually caused by flawed
infrastructure," said Alice. "Old power
plants and power lines need to be updated."

Grandpa loved to encourage Alice's
interest in science. But this time he snorted,
"Ha! It's the Light Catchers' fault. You've
heard of the Light Catchers, right?"

"I'm not in the mood for ghost stories, Grandpa," said Trevor. His grandpa loved telling tall tales.

"Please tell us, Grandpa," exclaimed Alice who also loved a good story. "Trevor is just a scaredy-cat."

"I am not a scaredy-cat! I want to hear the story, too," Trevor said nervously.

Grandpa Saul took Alice's flashlight and held it below his chin so the beam lit up his face. Grandpa looked frightening.

"Those pixie Light Catchers are only a few inches tall, but angry and mean. They look like tiny people, except with dragonfly wings and long stingers instead of noses. They steal light from street lamps and eat light. You see, it tastes like cupcakes to them. They suck light into their stingers and bring it home for their babies to eat."

Do you think we can find a Light Catcher if we go outside to look for one?" Alice asked excitedly.

Her grandfather shook his head. "They're nocturnal, so they only come out at night, and mostly avoid people if they can. But back when I was a young man, they were much bolder, buzzing around, chasing people, and eating light."

"Light is as valuable as water or food around here," Grandpa said. "I couldn't have these little pests stealing it, so I decided to catch one. In those days, there was a barn in the back of the house. One night, I left a candle glowing on a window ledge and hid. When one of those Light Catchers came for a nibble, I jumped out and caught that little fellow in a jar. That Light Catcher was so angry, but I just laughed and put the jar in the barn."

"The next evening, a huge horde of those night-loving pixies came and stole all the lights from a mile around. I grabbed a big butterfly net and spent the entire night chasing those angry creatures. They were fast, but after a few hours, I caught about a hundred and put them in jars in the barn. You should have seen that barn glow!"

"They should use some of those pixies at the power plant," said Alice, "With all their light, there would never be blackouts."

"You should never catch a Light Catcher," said Grandpa. "And I was about to find that out the hard way."

"The pixies were angry," continued Grandpa. "I couldn't get near the barn without hearing the Light Catchers yelling. I was scared to let them go; I didn't know what they'd do. But I decided that I couldn't keep them trapped any longer; it was just plain mean. So I went to the barn the next night to let them out."

"I should have been paying attention to the weather; I didn't realize a big storm had been blowing in. As soon as I approached the barn, I heard the wind howling. I had never seen a storm like that. The barn swayed, and the doors crashed open, and then, just like that, the walls blew away."

"Were the pixies OK? Tell me they were OK!" cried Alice.

"It's just a make-believe story," said Trevor, but then he added quietly, "They were OK, right, Grandpa?"

"You bet they were OK," said Grandpa Saul. "But the wind shattered all their jars. The pixies were buzzing around, charging at me with their stingers. They chased me all the way back to the house, and I barely made it back inside!"

"I could see the pixies outside eating all the lights around town. They weren't just hungry; they wanted to get me back for catching them. The next day, the newspaper reported high winds had knocked down some power lines, and the infrastructure had been torn to pieces, but I knew the truth. It was the pixies."

"But they didn't stop there. They were still mad and still hungry, and a few of them flew all the way up to the sun. They ate the sun's light and stored it inside their pointy stingers. All of Barrow fell into darkness.

"It took weeks for the sun to shine brightly again, and now, once a year, the pixies fly back up to the sun and steal the light, keeping it for two months, all because of what I did. It's dark every winter in Barrow because of those nocturnal pests. And that's why you should never try to catch a Light Catcher."

"That's the silliest story I've ever heard," said Trevor.

An electric noise filled the room, and all the lights came back on. Trevor looked out the window into the darkness and saw something glowing outside. He squinted to get a better look. He saw a winged creature with a long stinger looking back at him. But it couldn't be … could it?

"Is that a …" said Trevor, but as soon as he pointed, the creature flew away, if it had even been there at all. Trevor figured it must have been his imagination—maybe.

Check In   How did Grandpa Saul explain Alaska's seasonal light and dark periods?

Daylight Saving Time— PRO or CON?

by Jennifer Boudart

"Spring forward, fall back." This phrase reminds us to change our clocks twice each year for Daylight Saving Time (DST). The United States uses DST to allow for more daylight hours in summer and to save energy. Many people like DST and want to keep it, but others want to **abolish** it.

PRO

Life is better with Daylight Saving Time. Daylight Saving Time improves our family relationships and health. During DST, more people are active and spend time outdoors with their families.

DST makes us safer. During DST, people can travel home from work and school before dark. Driving conditions are safer before dark. A study published in 2007 showed that, in the last 30 years, traffic accidents fell six to ten percent during DST months. Crime rates fell, too.

DST saves energy. Fewer lights are needed when there are more hours of daylight. Studies show that on a national level, DST saves us enough energy each year to power about 100,000 households.

DST helps the environment. Much of our nation's electricity comes from burning coal, which pollutes the air.

Turning lights on later means fewer hours of artificial light. This reduces air and light pollution. It also improves life for **nocturnal** wildlife.

DST is good for the economy. Golf courses, recreation areas, and many stores see profits rise during DST.

These reasons support keeping Daylight Saving Time in the United States. It helps our society in many ways.

CON

Life is not better with Daylight Saving Time. Did you know our government does not **mandate** DST?

DST puts our health at risk. Health experts say our bodies do not adjust to gaining an extra hour of daylight. The change makes it more difficult for people to fall asleep. As a result, people sleep less and get sick more.

People in favor of DST say that daylight in the early evening hours improves driving safety. Yet people easily adjust to less light in the evenings in winter.

However, in winter, the sun sets before most people can drive home from work. This means it is dark when they drive to and from work.

DST can increase energy use. At night, DST can save energy on the national level. But recent studies show that in some local areas energy use increases in the morning, when it's dark.

DST hurts the economy. People think DST was started to help farmers, but farmers cannot change their work practices based on the clock. Farmers rise early. With DST, more of the morning is dark. Farmers have less daylight in their workday.

These reasons support ending the practice of Daylight Saving Time. DST does not improve our quality of life.

Check In With which side do you agree? Why?

Discuss Concepts and Ideas

1. What connections can you make among the three pieces in *Catch the Light*? How are the pieces related?

2. Compare the information you learned in the science article, "Bright Lights Have a Dark Side," with the information you learned in the opinion piece. How is the information alike and different?

3. What is the relationship between artificial light and light pollution?

4. What did you visualize when Grandpa Saul told his story about the Light Catchers? Did the illustrations match the picture in your mind?

5. What reasons and evidence were most persuasive in the opinion piece? Did you change your opinion after reading both sides, pro and con? Why or why not?

6. What questions do you still have about natural and artificial light?